The Exile Letters

Daniel Raven

I'll wait for you,
As always.
Again in this forever

Cover Art by : Alyssa Batchie   (Instagram) @abatchieart

Cover Design by Anthony D Delaurentiis

CONTENTS

Exile lives in all of us, hidden in the vast depths of ones soul. In fact, we all start out this way don't we? Alone in the dark, with only the faint, muffled echoing of the outside world intruding our slumber. We cope, we adapt. Eventually we free ourselves from such isolation to meet and greet the obstacles to come. It's all a test is it not? Time skips on, slithering towards nothingness. Or perhaps there's something more. Hidden in the crevices of the soul that present itself in the end. A choice, a fork, an impasse on your way to redemption, resurrection, and finally…

Back into exile.

In every field of burden,
There is a dream.

Welcome to the diseased.
The dried and swollen.
The walking hidden façade of your former self.
An illusion,
 Nothing more.
Where those who think fate is purgatory and dreams are the end.

When my thoughts are empty,
 and my glass is full.
I sit quietly somber in the silence of it all,
 and watch the dying ghost of you,
 lean and pale fade from my memory.
Like little shards of glass,
 and shapeless mass
 cascading down my window,
Like the rain.

She haunts me to the point of altered.
By fate or consequence,
 These inner murmurs of a devout, promising voice once cherished
 and elated.
Now fall on dying embers beneath my memories stark embrace.

Perhaps in the margins of darkness,
Beneath the crevices deep.
Is where I'll convene with you my love,
And we can finally sleep.

Down deep through this wickedness treason,
Where life just seems but a dream.
Are all the pitfalls of vigor my love,
All that ceases to scream.

So should you perplex to see its heart,
Or even touch on its mien.
Tis where the devil resides my love,
His home beneath dirt and the leaves.

Pleasures always die first.
Then dreams,
 And when they've sunk deep into the abyss.
Fear comes out to play.

This empty roadway manifested soothes my callused feet.
Its cold concrete runs fast and deep,
 And still there's miles before I sleep,
Before these tired bones shall reap,
 And then my souls sequestered.

Head north, always north.
Four folgers packets and a cup a noodles only get you so far.
Sirens stopped.
Don't mean shit, could be a trap.
Whole worlds a trap now.
Still.
Cant stay here.

Barren
Empty
Landscape.

You can almost hear the voices of them children in the play yard.
Giggling, trippin in the dirt.
Faint smell of bbq and dog feces.
Was a time in August you couldn't walk a block or two in either
 direction without ingestin all 12 courses through your lungs.
That is,
Before the end.
Get up old man, shake it off.

North.

Even if I held steady this sinking ship.
The rutter would rust eventually,
 And drown the very reason I kept afloat.

The worlds a tattered coffee table,
 Dressed up like a stage.
Give me innocence,
Give me farouche,
Give me unhinged existentialism,
Give me cerebral enlightenment.
Show me another face,
 And another.
We're all just a carousel of cautious children.
Still afraid of the dark.

Ain't no absolution in attrition,
Ain't no substance.
No straight and narrow,
No black,
          Or white.
Not even gray.
Just mist.
Just apparitions of ether,
 And the manumit of immaculate peace.

Vision seeks out what it wants,
 Then turns blind.
Sought through sacred circumstances.
Infrequent movement,
 And hedged opaque clarity.
Till the window fills with years of dust,
 And grit,
 And faded cracks.
Yet the center lies newborn smooth.

Can't save her.
Why try?
Persistent bastard.

    Obdurate.

Ends the same.
Why rewrite the beginning?
Always the same.
Desperate oath,
 Think that makes you human?
Makes you somebody?
No fault here,
 Only fate,
        And you can't kill that which you know longer believe in.

Discordant vapors seem to soothe my hollowed heart.
Through the windy corridors of veins that catalog my misery.
Vested champions of ingress.
May heaven or hell wander through such spoor less grief.
Guilt ways such upon my perennial malediction and cuts a shape out of
 The dark form of the world.
Should one wrench my sin from its seed and stand before me beating
 True,
        Like the glow of an angel.
Gentle to the touch.
I fear I may weep in her presence.
Unprepared for all her love and virtue.

Sometimes I dream of us,
 Far into the future.
In a small town in the Midwest.
Nehawka Nebraska.
Near the weeping water creek.
Where the wind smells clean and chaste.
The two of us on the porch,
 Untouched by the world.
Your legs wrapped in an old blanket we found when we moved in.
The walls filled with photographs of your likeness,
 But none of them are you.
Us.
The pasts long been dead and buried,
 And the open azure sky excepts us warmly.
Granting us amnesty among the little macrocosm we've created.

Holding her down by the edge of the bed,
  I made her feel my violence.
 Hands on her neck,
  Shunting blood south.
Assaulting the night with perpetual cadence.
Pacing her heart.
Sheets entangled,
  Sediment of my seed already on her lips
                    I wait.
For her eyes to fade,
  And her lips to purse and curve with the slightest of surrender.
Then pardon her throat before filling her fertile void.

As faint and weak as a thought.
This bleeding logic
 Shall become an end,
 An enigma,
                An abyss that will swallow all of me,
 And scatter like dust,
 Like strange property among the stars.

Her lips were astonishingly supple for an oppressor of indulgence.
A quality that spanned the length of her thighs,
 And bore a fragrance familiar to patrician.

My heart suffers from a detestable slackness with regard to the rest of my
  Forgiving organs.

A deceptive longing only defaces
 This detrimental heart.
Singular in matter.
Yet properly corruptible to the many who violate its trust.

Oh how I long for a correlation communion.
Tongues entangled in serenity.
Fingers exploring in the dark.

Can love sometimes occur without pain or misery?
In these fallen cities,
 Beyond the flame char sky.
Where our haunts torment and provoke such spiritual shudder.
Out of reach of such juxtapose.
Would it be worth living?

Keep the monster at bay.
Push it deep.
Send it back.
Swallow it whole.
Now smile,
            And shake his hand.

The dark follows me.
A rainbow of misery.
A menagerie of meaningless suitors,
 Who help sew my morning cloak of will.

I've become an accomplice in my own existence.
Longing for the darkness.
Hiding from the truth of the world.
The fevered dream,
 A frozen spectator.
Watching innocents hold back a legion of horribles
 Inches from the fray,
                    As I lay,
SWOLLEN,

With new hindsight.

Dare to dream immaculate.
 Past insignificant martyrs.
        Knee
        Deep
            In the mire.
 It's how its gotta be.
 This life ain't pretty.
 These souls ain't soulless.
 Preachers preach,
  Bankers bitch.

        Words.

 Pick your poison, lay it out.
 Stark,
  Like an instinct.
 Find your peace and swig.
 All them other deities can wait.

How long have I been asleep?
Full blown out rapid eye movement.
Heavy slumber, drug induced sleep.
Ambien existence.
How long have I been walking around in this skull of mine.
Circling the drain.
Lap after lap of self evasive masturbation of the senses.
An on going carousel of nothingness,
 Gray matter.
The absolute absolute.
No map.
Oblivious.
Another day another hobby.
Chew the fat,
 Join a cause,
 Is any of this really helping?

Owned by this beautiful nightmare,
 I reprieve.
Through the cobble stone corridors,
 Anchored in sin.
Unable to forgive.
Unquenched by fortitude.
A dead man.
Frozen between solace and discord at every turn.
For what may lie ahead I can not bear.
Whether it be in this soul or the next,
 My heart retreats.
Stoic in a box.
Eternal.

Underneath these tattered bones is a graveyard of antiquity.

She walked along the bottom of my adrenaline dump.
Thwarting my lips underlying propensity for violence,
 And right there,
 Exposed in the moment.
Without walls.
I was left to curl up in the fetal position and write my own obituary.

How could you sway so sinfully into my sovereignty.
Beyond my lock and key.
Nestled in the center of my heart and anima,
 You listen to me breathe.

Who is she anyway?
 She always been knockin around this skull.
 Concussing my sight,
  Altering my now.
 Why she always around?
 Visitin in my dark,
  Hauntin my virtue,
  Scoldin my sinin ways.
 Why she always preechin?
 Openin that pretty mouth,
  Showin all her hate,
  Right down to the gums.
 She ain't never been invited.
 I don't remember openin my door.
 Runnin, walkin,
                    She always three steps behind.
 Like some naggin geisha.
 I give up.
 You ain't never leavin is you?
 Like a tic up in the skin.
 Brusin me from the inside.
 Tired.
 Dragin my shell around with you harrassin.
 Make yourself useful and grab us a shovel.
 Heaven awaits just around the bend.

I know not where you are my sweet,
 Or who you'll cease to be.
I only know I search for you,
 Forever in my dreams.

Its such significant failure that drives this niche of despondency.

No matter how much you want to give her sight.
Set her free.
Take her pain and christen it your own.
You can never be,
          Her comfort.

I grab it firmly from the shelf,
 My nightly ritual.
A wet and calming oasis in my desert of confusion.
Two cubes and pour.
A non-newtonian viscoelastic fluid,
 Yet just as vital for sustainment.
Sanity.
I hide it, and it hides me.
Shuts me off from the rest of the world.
As I lie peacefully in its bosom.
If only for a couple of hours before the dawn.

What's wrong my warrant?
Has your lust perceived?
Was it yours at all?
Or has your mind believed?

Sanguine such thoughts I beg of you.
Vanquish this skin that you see.
Try once more to live.
Try once more to be free.

Dream a dream immaculate,
 Far better than those who may see.
My love, my life, my everything,
 Who beckons the air that I breathe.
Who owns the very air that I breathe.

Dream a dream near farther than those who dare to dream.
To hold the very one you love encased in reverie.
To own that night in time to right to ever be it seen.
That all is lost to open eyes when mornings sun is deemed.

Forsaken are we.
Forsaken and alone with hindrance held upon the past indifferences of
 Memory.
Faded like the wants and dreams of yesterday.
I want to see,
             Breathe,
                     Touch,
                             Taste the very absence of you.
Cleanse my scars with salt.
You move through me like cold wind and I cannot cease before the very
 Reckoning perverts my soul.

I want you.

Just you and only you.
Whole and untainted in my arms.
Naïve and innocent and naked as the day.
Flesh against flesh.
No secrets,
           No lies,
                   No sin.
A tryst blood deep
Staked in fertile soil
Wet with virile life in pools of cloudy water.
Organic nurtured love.
My fetish lingers long.
Harboring shapes, grieving comfort.
Like a lost child blind of the world.
Blank as the idea before.
Full as the pages that follow.
For one must lead the other until the very end.

You reckon its fate then?
Why we's here now,
 An not before?
Blind fate.
Like we ain't got no choice in the matter.
Earth just turns.
Free men, chained men,
 Dead men.
The world takes.
A vast and endless alternative.
Binds us, smothers us,
 Blankets us with options.
Falsity.
The falsity of illusion is in its coldness.
The stillness of its calm can quake the very center of a man.
Leave his guts on the floor,
 And his heart in the ice box.

She leaves only words in her wake,
   And the dull sting of despondency.

Cannot stop thinking about you.
Your smile.
Your elegant eyes.
Your soft billowy lips.
The nape of your neck.
The very shape of your curves and how I could spend all day
 Curled up inside them.
Inside you.
Your scent.
Your breath on mine.
Your moan.
Your playful retreat from my assault of neck kisses.
Your weight on my lap.
The way you'd lay your hand in mine and mingle with my fingers.
Your laugh.
Your giggle.
Your morning kiss and naked walk to the bathroom.
Your tiny goose bumps in the shower.
Your everything,
                    Every time I close my eyes.

This raw life
Leads on in sickness.
Through the jagged cobblestones.
Past dreams,
Past hope,
Past the last stop this train has to offer.
Dragging this lifeless sack of meat.
Relying on inertia

G
R
A
V
I
T
Y

Praying for momentum.
Determined.
Focused
       On solace.

These desperate oaths.
Hallowed rituals,
Rancid relics of the past.
As this eternal night endures it seethes with a quietness.
Solemn as a church,
Deadly as a sorrow.

All love is a ruse.
A flattering figment.
Give up.
 Enjoy singular peace.

When last we spoke
Your lips were deafening,
 And my hands
Trembled though you could not see.
The two of us,
 One whole.
Unvaccinated by suspicion under the mother moon.

When we kiss I can taste the monstrous fecundity of your loins.

This heart.
Heavy and unwanted,
Has here by been tucked back into oblivion.

Our two paths couldn't be further apart.
Yet I still dream of you
 In fields of flagrant ambivalence.
You are a dream,
A mythos.
An antiquated visage of my soul.
An uprising of my insides,
 Foretelling the foretold through a twisted rhythm my heart
 Cannot decipher.

Pale,
My body subsists and sustains itself.
Like an ineffectual phantom,
 Floating on a hill of my transgressions.

Here I stand haughty and erect.
A drunken degenerate,
 Deformed by the past.
Scared by trust.
An unforgiven amongst this pavements treachery.

My eyes seek repose in those melting graces,
Those translucent shades of brown.

We shall walk again.
Hand in hand
 Along the cusp of memory.
Our oaths valued with remembrance.
A time capsule hidden within my synapses.
Protected.
Sheltered from the tears of the sun.

Before your lips can even part,
  Your eyes drip with ultimatums.

Leave the monster
 Advance into the thick.
For I am baptized.
A walking symbol of banishment.
A pride never to be satisfied.
A love never to be whole.

I met love once.
 She was tiny
  And unopposed in her beauty.
 But she cut like a banshee
  And left me to bleed out on the linoleum.

Fate has arranged for me an almost unbearable feast of
   Quandary's
         Vexations
               And other arbitrary accouterments.

At night she walks like prose.
 An impulse of my desire
          Yet
 Always out of reach.

Between the breaths and moans,
Between the gasps and groans,
Between the touch and absence.
My mind oscillates the nights pendulum.
The results of which
  Manifest itself in the morning.

Without you there is no me.
If you are gone I cannot breathe.

The dream continues.
 I follow blindly
  Through the stories syntax.
 I chase her.
 Beyond every dark hallway presented.
 Till her symmetry reveals herself to me at first light,
  And together we melt in the corner.

Guide me through this labyrinth of layered lust.
For I am a disheveled old man with a candle.
Obliged by oddities,
Sunk by suppleness.
Bound by exquisite restraints
                              Take me.
Lead me on through my graces.
To the alter of perpetual triumph and sacrifice.

Hindsight lives in me,
 To strong to ever leave,
 To quick of wit
  Yet laced with strife
 To blind to ever see.

My exodus returns,
But free from welts or burns,
Instead it rips
 And tears apart
My fleeting faint concerns.

Till I no longer care,
My thoughts my feelings bare,
A soulless ghost
 A paupers prize
Forgone from lifes repair.

The memory evokes.
Leads on.
Vial and blackened,
Rotisserie dripping with ripening irony.
Visions upon visions
 Like ocular symphonies.
All akin to establish the contemptuous epithet of my youth.
A once full and hearty soul
             Now barren by memories to heavy to harbor in this skull.

Faithful to nothing but the arduous day,
I shall be a beast for the remainder.

If it were meant so it would be.
　A curious paradox
　　　　　　The heart.
It holds the key to infinite possibilities.
The brain steers the vessel but surely the heart is its captain.
Wise, rogue oracle.
All feeling.
　　　　All learning allusive algebraist of the soul.

Skies in heat today.
Every time it opens its mouth it shows red.
Like what flesh is to bone.
High rolling,
 Patiently passing.
Its breath gentle on the downside.
Its presence slight.
Like a papercut.
The sky reaches all.
Touch the day,
Open your mouth
          Pass through.

Diners open.
Neon's on.
Depressives
 Insomniacs
  Lonely hearts
Drunkards.
The desolate and destitute.
Were all here,
 Waiting on the specials.
Pull up a seat,
 Take the corner.
Suns peering,
                    Displaying dust like a living carousel.
Steaks tuff,
 Eggs runny,
Tabs always on me.

If you love someone let them go
  Something
  Something
  Blah
      Blah
        Blah
            Pass the scotch.

Like a child in full discovery.
Like a Brahminy kite.
Placid
Perched HIGH upon a promontory.

You save me.

The moon suspends us,
The light intrigues,
The clouds endure,
The air it bleeds,
The night it soothes,
The grass it breathes,
The heart it wants,
The soul it sees.

The abyss of my history,
Lines on my face.
Proud roads of poverty.
Cracks,
Holes.
No shoulder.
Gritty and un governed.
A palpable map of loss.
Where my thoughts go to grieve.

Just as the willowed moon holds its presence in the night,
  Shelters all the wood from eternal equinox.
  So shall my dying heart,
                        With you.

Live you bastard live!
Pick your teeth up,
 Throw that armor away

Wont need it.

Go on, lead with your head.
Lean in.
          Get close.
Two to the cage ought to do.
Drag that prize home.
Bathe in its blood.
Smile you caw,
 Victory.

Reaching
Retched
Regal lengths of cerebral debauchery takes a steady hand,
 And a full glass,
 And often ends with
Lurid
Lengthy
Loquacious fulminating protests with the linoleum.

I dream of a pristine awakening.
A collaboration of the euphoric at the moment of acceptance.
Negating all time and space.
An infinitesimal, arbitrary, Norse soliloquy.
Kneaded beneath the earth with the roots.
Awaiting flight to Valhalla.

Wish I knew what's next.
No rhythm to it,
 Its all gumbo.
Scattered cuts of meat,
      Rendered fat.
We want,
  We take
   We own
    We lose.
Boil, simmer

R
E
D
U
C
E.

This room.

        These walls.

This perdition persists on pushing the very envelope of my patience.

They sit in silence and judge,

Eggshell stained,

          Of white ocular protagonists of scrutiny.

        DESISIT!

Hold your hollow perspicacity somewhere else.

What do you know of the world?

Solid pillars

 Nothing more.

You shall listen to me type, and speak, and rant.

Retain my tears,

 Absorb my blows just as those before me.

Now watch me poor another you horrid gauge of habitation.

All at once,
 Like ethereal fire,
I want to be tied up in you.
Your lips
Your arms
The blanket
The bed
Every swollen inch.

The unhinged intoxication of you.
Unstable as a dream.
I pray I never wake.

Father time,
 Have you not the slightest access to ease the afforded of pain?
 A grace I have prayed upon in every epithet known to me, only
 To wake up nightly with tainted lust.

This road ends soon.
Turn in your invincibility.
Fears,
      Passions.
Anything human.
Provides the opportunity for self admiration.
A façade,
           The man who thinks.
Time to mash the petal.
Throw the last 10 into the wheel.
Grin you sonofabitch
 Your free.
Taste the heat from the engine block.
Let it soak deep in the bone.
Feel that existential quandary,
 And don't you ever
                Look away.

I sit in this empty room without her.
Nothingness surrounds.
Stale,
        Fragrant emptiness.
Where the hopeless harvest heartache,
 And the loudest always screams in silence.   .

Feats or famine.
One more horrid then the other.
Cheat or starve.
Where's your God now?
He's broken you.
Owned.
High in the heavens lies salvation.
Down in the dirt lies you.
A face,
   A will.
A dirty Pagan with blood on his hands.
Boot deep.
Wading in the worlds hypocrisy.

Desperate oaths sewn deep
 Drain the meek
Like a swollen tic.

Beyond the hall of broken hearts
 Where bones lay loose on fleshy parts
And sin chases down the dark province of night.

It's impulse now that gets us all
 Like sweeping leaves long after fall
And yet her mere trace
                    Is all that prevents my anarchy.

My Dear Eidolon,

Invisible, indivisible muse. I have no corpus long. Only tattered fragments.
They cast a vale of soul making, as virtue stirs the pulp, (crowds my
anxiety). Time to move on through the pathos. Whiskey, beer. Licit, illicit.
Its death must enter backwards.

Our love bordered the rhetoric.
An exalted denunciation of the heart.
A sullied oblivion,
 A living system of exchanges involving a sensuous abundance
 Of dominant
                    Bodily rhythms.
Prodigious presence.
Insurmountable passion.
Empty promise.

I would have given my life.
Gouged my heart out from its cage and burned it to cinder
 with all the other memories. Till it lay a sanguine ashen relic of the past.
I would have done this, pure and simple.
For one more night in her arms.

This insipid ache.
Dilates and disseminates every vessel.
Bone deep.
Taking all that's reserved for sustainment.
So intense as to border absolution.
May I never again have recourse to such a malignant savior.
When next fate chides me.
Decides to crush my heart.
I pray it finishes the job entirely.

I live for tomorrow.
As the night grows long, and silent.
I await your whisper in the dark.

Compel thy heart to contemplate thy beauty.
Where in the foolish only take delight,
 But the humble, and deserved,
 Savior as a gift.

Her skin was like silk and bore an electrical charge unlike any common
Angel known to man. It was there, in her embrace I learned to live again.

Partake of this soul.
This fog of remembrance.
Life's as crooked as a jigsaw.
Never lose true north, fall prey to the broodish.
Beyond these clouded judgments there is only truth.
Has to be.
Only something so complicated could be that simple.

My temperance dies in your embrace.
My fears falter.
My soul weeps.
My body weakens.
My thoughts erase,
 And my will retreats within.

To often I have let this heart instruct.
            Guide.
Mentor my affections.
How anemic these eyes evaluate the past.
They blur and bludgeon.
Tear the tangible from the abstract.
Then murder indiscriminately.
Like buckshot in the wind.

Life's a series of wasted moments
False truths
                And witty banter.
We all gotta fill the hole somehow.
Question is,
 You fill yours with a shovel?
Or a spoon?

I will never forget you.
Even when this heart stops beating
 And these lungs stop breathing.
I will live on,
   Through you.

Wintery night,
Sex on my fingers,
Snow gently genuflecting to the moon
 before bequeathing to the pavement.
Record skips and screams epiphany.
Secretly showing me our dream.

This grit will
 not be grout.
      I wont let it.
      In time, it will dissolve.

Dear sky,

    Where do we end?
    Is there still room between them stars?

        I want to believe.

    This hedonist heart haunts my state of grace,
     I swear it.
    Suddle as a tack hammer.
    How long must I wait beneath the earth,
     Till mercy come and grant
                me
                 peace.

This iris haunts
 As my mind mumbles reverberations of this soul.
Both cavernous and obtuse.
It hosts my deepest miseries.
Serving them tea in the dark.

How often have I built this shelter,
  Only to lie on its roof and bask in the moonlight.

Go on!

Take   The   Key!

You're gonna need some semtex

And a

T
I
G   welder

To get to this [HEART].

I keep you always and forever
Tucked away in a tiny pocket in the corner of my mind.
The one that smells of missionary and scotch,
 And on the eve of forgetfulness I sully the pocket once more.
With my minds foul,
                    flagrant,
                                fingers,
 and brace for insurrection.

Certain thoughts chase you through life.
But none more potent then "what if"...

The truth of silence seems lost through this labyrinth of cruelty.
If ever mercy walked among us,
 She would tremble at the sight.
        Stained.
Her errant wings could never sustain such confession.

Winds waitin,
 Plottin.
Planning to swoop down n steal my breath.
Sudden like a shot.
Pierce your chest n freeze your ventricles.
Hold'em there raw,
 Exposed.
Like they was on trial for abandonment.

My one true memory,
My hymn,
My nightly ritual.
Help me sleep again.
Help me convalesce what's left of this dying heart.

I will not bend to the natural decay of things.
This heart will hold sway over this fold,
 And the next.
Until I find you again.

It shall take both daring prudence and non reaction of every conceivable tendency to cover the space that looms between us. Many a soul has lost on this battlefield. His heart extinguished for life.

Lie with me in black satin,
Under the harvest moon,
Where all of our inhibitions,
Are displayed right there in bare bloom.

I,
Directly distinguished
But benign from intelligence.
A revenant of neither seething matter
Nor query of intellect.
Must rely on the abstract of enigma within,
To find my beating heart.

I could fall asleep for a thousand years dreaming,
  And still not find the happiness I feel when I'm with you.

In order to understand "a way" you must have knowledge of its birth.
Its center.
        Living but long forgotten.
Like the ruminants of myth buried in libraries.
Its message is sleeping.

This great wall of memory.
Primitively expressed
 Response less
  And dragged through a thousand darkness's
Can never achieve solace.

You all suppose we got a number?
Like at the deli.
Mean,
We ain't nothing but big sacks a meat anyways.
Grandpapa's preachin bout them crows again.
Says,
Bad omen.
They ain't never cut my soul.
They ain't never force the bottle on me.
Turn me blind.
Hold my foot in reverse and lay little Ahanu to rest.
I reckon it's cold beneath the grass.
 All those uncertainties.
Least up here,
          I can feel the sun.

You fuel me,
You comfort me,
You drain me lifeless and leave me lusting for more.

She was a wonderful coincidence.
An ephemeral moment of delight.
I replay every moment spent.
From the smallest of gestures,
 To the demonstrative press of her lips on mine.
My minds response to the nights insensibility.

Before the weeds surrounded our atheism.
 Choked the dirt from our teeth
  You should know,
  It was freedom.
 Pure
        And simple,
 And before the air left my lungs eternal,
 I knew it so.

Drops of bloody agony
    Flow
       From this disenchanted heart.
Like an emblem of grief.

This night beats life under your forgiving shadow,
 And when the moon reaches the witching hour
 Your dark form reveals to me the altruism of this world.
If only for a moment.
If only for this moment out of all.
I have touched God.

My hearts insurrection can not contain these tears.
When next we meet,
This soulless mountain shall gain in glory,
A loveless peace.

Repentant of the irrevocable
These weak wounds
 Received in hospitality,
Only honor the infamous
Through vain idolatry,
                    And evil in God.

My fears fornicate in the dark.
 They mix with liquor
  And the hazard of inestimable loss.
 Loud they grow through expeditious parliament.
 They feed the monster within.

Long have I questioned this vestal star.
Its magnetic might.
Its purity.
The way it sits between heaven and hell,
 nurturing its circumference
                                    with light.

While she invited dull morality with every sweet soft gesture of her lips.
I felt my body surrender to her sorcery.

Hear that undulating murmur in my chest?
 It leaves my skin pale
  And pupils fixed.
 It traps the hope of you
        Of us,
 Within this pregnant heart.

At first she lived,
As others lived
Among the strange and merry.
Awaiting her breathing soul,
Her hearts encounters a countless many.

BUT

Melancholy
Melancholy
Came softly through the night.
It bade her breath
Awoke her fear
And with one sweet kiss,
It took her very sight.

AND

Now she waits,
As others wait,
For worlds to end and die.
For tears to shed
And hearts to bleed
 And others to ponder why.

In my prison lies a populous
 Of interspersed
                    Trepidation.
Every time I think of you.

My nightly visits
 Bloom in this hallway of solace.
 Where even form
 Is abstract,
 And winsome bliss
 Is but another
   Shaded mystery.

    Ought,
Or ought not.
Seems trivial.
In the end the devils waiting for your body to quit.
So your two fathers can commence with the war for your soul.

Each alteration of my wounded heart
Promotes partial death.
Till I am no more than a walking shell
Of human atrocities.

Oh love,
How I chase you.
Despite your mortal sting.
My hearts a sanguine hue,
My mind a fallen king.

Those eyes.
Her eyes.
A listless lethargy of sadness,
In this temporary forever.

You are in every word I write.
In every thought I have,
 Your presence owns them all.
Like a slave to the dawn,
Without you I can't breathe.

Our souls,
They speak in truths
Of what can,
And cannot be.
Of everything that was,
And things that still will be.
Why ask why within,
When you already know.
Our souls are intertwined,
Without one they cannot glow.

I refuse to give up on this inevitable...

ABOUT THE AUTHOR

Daniel Raven is a noted poet/writer that resides in Sleepy Hollow NY. The Exile Letters is his first published collection of poetry.

Made in the USA
Lexington, KY
24 July 2016